T0413365

STEM

The Battle between 2-D and 3-D

Shapes

Georgia Beth

Consultants

Lisa Ellick, M.A.
Math Specialist
Norfolk Public Schools

Pamela Estrada, M.S.Ed.
Teacher
Westminster School District

Publishing Credits

Rachelle Cracchiolo, M.S.Ed., *Publisher*
Conni Medina, M.A.Ed., *Managing Editor*
Dona Herweck Rice, *Series Developer*
Emily R. Smith, M.A.Ed., *Series Developer*
Diana Kenney, M.A.Ed., NBCT, *Content Director*
Stacy Monsman, M.A., *Editor*
Kristy Stark, M.A.Ed., *Editor*
Kevin Panter, *Graphic Designer*

Image Credits: All images from iStock and/or Shutterstock

Teacher Created Materials
5301 Oceanus Drive
Huntington Beach, CA 92649-1030
http://www.tcmpub.com

ISBN 978-1-4258-5823-0
© 2018 Teacher Created Materials, Inc.
Made in China
Nordica.112017.CA21701237

Table of Contents

Welcome! 4

Round 1 8

Round 2 12

Round 3 16

Round 4 23

And the Winner Is… 26

Problem Solving 28

Glossary 30

Index... 31

Answer Key.. 32

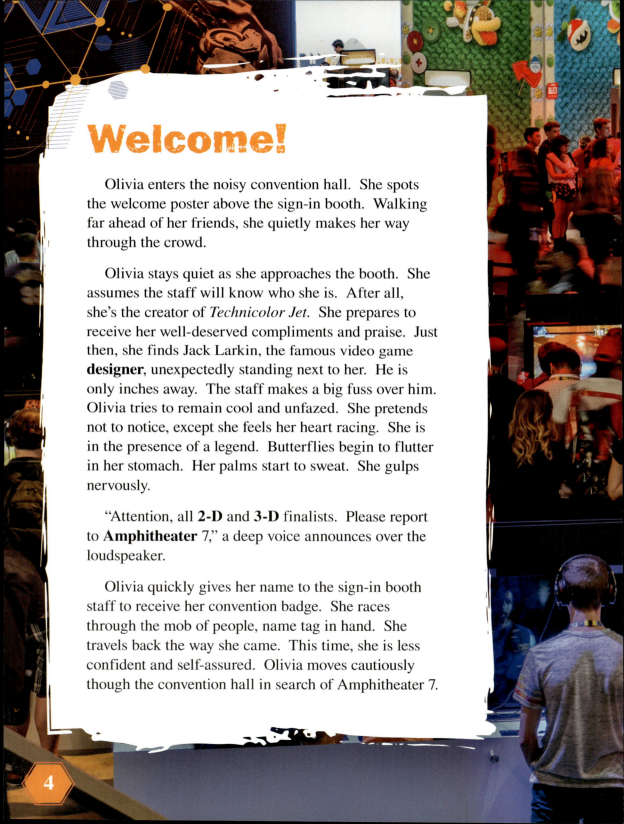

Welcome!

Olivia enters the noisy convention hall. She spots the welcome poster above the sign-in booth. Walking far ahead of her friends, she quietly makes her way through the crowd.

Olivia stays quiet as she approaches the booth. She assumes the staff will know who she is. After all, she's the creator of *Technicolor Jet*. She prepares to receive her well-deserved compliments and praise. Just then, she finds Jack Larkin, the famous video game **designer**, unexpectedly standing next to her. He is only inches away. The staff makes a big fuss over him. Olivia tries to remain cool and unfazed. She pretends not to notice, except she feels her heart racing. She is in the presence of a legend. Butterflies begin to flutter in her stomach. Her palms start to sweat. She gulps nervously.

"Attention, all **2-D** and **3-D** finalists. Please report to **Amphitheater** 7," a deep voice announces over the loudspeaker.

Olivia quickly gives her name to the sign-in booth staff to receive her convention badge. She races through the mob of people, name tag in hand. She travels back the way she came. This time, she is less confident and self-assured. Olivia moves cautiously though the convention hall in search of Amphitheater 7.

A small crowd awaits the start of a competition in a dark amphitheater.

The contestants take a long escalator to an underground amphitheater. A small crowd of gamers looks on. Jack and Olivia take their places on the raised area at the center of the stage.

The **emcee** begins, "Welcome to the National Gaming Challenge. Today's competition is between the finalists of the 2-D and 3-D categories. Jack Larkin will create two-dimensional video games, and Olivia Kuan will work in three-dimensional virtual reality. There will be four rounds of competition. Each round will focus on a different shape. Whoever creates the best games will win and…become the new reigning champion!"

Visions of classic video games flash in Jack's head. His old favorites always come to mind whenever it is time to design a new game.

Olivia begins chewing her gum in slow motion. Her mind, though, is moving at lightning speed. She silently vows to create something that no one has ever imagined.

"Do you accept this challenge?" the emcee asks Jack and Olivia.

"I do," they both answer. They give each other a quick glance.

"Then, let the games begin," the emcee declares to the audience. "Competition will start tomorrow. Tonight, have some dinner and meet new people. Good luck to you both!".

LET'S EXPLORE MATH

Jack designs classic 2-D games. Identify the polygons used in the characters below.

Round 1

That night Jack stays up late trying to prepare. In the morning, he moans at the piercing sound of the alarm, but he's proud of what he's created. He is excited and ready to wow the convention crowd.

During Round 1, Jack shares his game, *Burst the Bubble*, with the audience. More importantly, he shares it with the panel of judges. Judges start the game and are greeted with a satisfying pop and a dreamy series of bubbles. Then, they pop bubbles to travel through an underwater world. Soon, bubbles appear faster, forming dense clouds that are easy to get lost in.

"I'm almost there!" a judge yelps, his thumb jumping furiously on the controller. Looking on, Olivia pops her gum carelessly. But, she is worried. The judge looks like he has completely fallen for the game.

"They're just bubbles, but I could play this all day!" he exclaims, finally putting the controller down. "How did you do it?"

"The game takes advantage of the progress **principle**," Jack replies. "Players want to keep playing when they feel like they are making progress."

"It doesn't hurt that you're testing reaction times," Olivia adds.

"That's on purpose. I love speed games because they get my heart pumping," says Jack.

"It looks like the judges love them, too," Olivia admits to herself.

LET'S EXPLORE MATH

Suppose that one of the challenges in *Burst the Bubble* is to pop bubbles containing quadrilaterals. Choose all of the bubbles that players should pop.

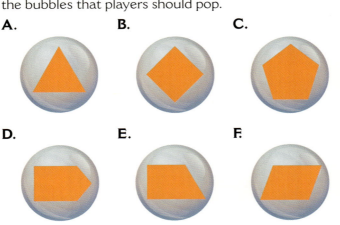

A.   B.   C.

D.   E.   F.

"You're going to be great," Jack says to Olivia. "I watched clips from your **portfolio**, and I'm impressed."

Olivia flashes a grateful smile. She syncs a customized headset with the screen so that the audience can watch. Then, she gives the headset to the judge who volunteered to play the game.

Soon, the view on-screen shifts from the competition **logo** to the sky to the atmosphere. An avatar of Olivia is seen floating past the moon and the **crystalline** rings of Saturn.

The audience gasps as a comet blazes on-screen. Then, the judge's avatar appears. It lands on Jupiter. The planet automatically **emits** a bright glow. The avatar quickly launches back into space. He floats past Neptune as the screen grows dark except for a few tiny **interstellar** points of light, while the planets glow faintly in the background.

The crowd cheers.

The judge pulls off the headset and sets it aside. He looks around to remind himself he is on solid ground.

"Olivia, it's evident you're a brilliant designer. But, Jack is the winner of this round," the judge says. "I found *Across the Universe* stunning but very overwhelming. I didn't know how to control the game. I was scared I would be lost in space forever!"

A judge gazes into space on his headset.

Olivia problem solves to create something new.

Round 2

When Olivia gets home, she is still disappointed. Once again, she has the challenge of creating something the world has never seen. But, she faces the constant threat of her game being labeled as "too bold," "too creative," or "too scary." She settles into her chair and begins to code. She must persevere.

Olivia works all night. The result of her work is *Mountain Climber*. The game requires players to master skills such as teamwork, map reading, climbing, and avoiding avalanches.

The next day, the judges put on their headsets. They hear the wind whistling, see 30-foot icicles crashing around them, and feel as though they are out of breath as they struggle to **ascend** a steep mountain.

"That was close," one judge utters after dropping a pickax.

But Olivia knows bigger challenges are ahead. The judges must keep their full attention on the game to avoid disaster.

Jack lets out a low whistle as he watches one of the judge's fellow climbers plummet off an icy cliff. "It's like a roller coaster where you can't see the track ahead of you!" the judge tells Olivia. "I love that."

Olivia grins. "Maybe this won't be a complete waste of time after all," she thinks.

MOUNTAIN CLIMBER

A hiker battles wind and ice atop a mountain.

"Ready to show us your design, Jack?" a judge asks.

"Absolutely." Jack hands the judge a controller and says, "I present to you *Kite-i-vation*."

The judge begins to explore the world of hang gliding. She adjusts the kite wings, takes a running start, and leaps out over the ocean. "I'm flying!"

The music gets louder as the judge rises into the sky. As the clouds envelop her and then reveal the earth from greater heights, even the oldest judges on the panel lean forward. "Everyone dreams of being a bird," Jack whispers to Olivia.

But it's not long before the judge sets aside the controller. "It's **mesmerizing**, but it feels more like a movie than a game. There's not much to do except look at the scenery, and there's no tension. No…no challenge," she says, smiling at Olivia.

"Maybe adding a few surprises would help keep players interested," Olivia offers.

"Excellent idea," says Jack.

Jack does not need the judges to tell him who the winner is. He scribbles ideas in his notebook; he doesn't want to be on the losing side again during the next round.

A hang glider shifts his weight to turn the glider in a smooth circle.

In *Kite-i-vation*, players use kites to explore surroundings. In mathematics, kites are quadrilaterals with 2 pairs of equal-length sides that are adjacent to, or beside, each other. They are not parallelograms, which have 2 pairs of opposite, equal-length, parallel sides. Sort the shapes into two groups: examples of parallelograms and non-examples of parallelograms.

Round 3

"I'm expecting extraordinary things from you." A judge's final words echo in Jack's head on Day 3 of the competition. He appreciates the trust that the judges have placed in him, and he doesn't want to disappoint them. Plus, he'd like the opportunity to teach Olivia a few things and show her up.

By the time the judges all take their seats, Jack is ready with a video game that is inspired by his childhood and his love of classic games.

"It's called *Shadow Eater,*" Jack announces. "I hope you like it as much as I do."

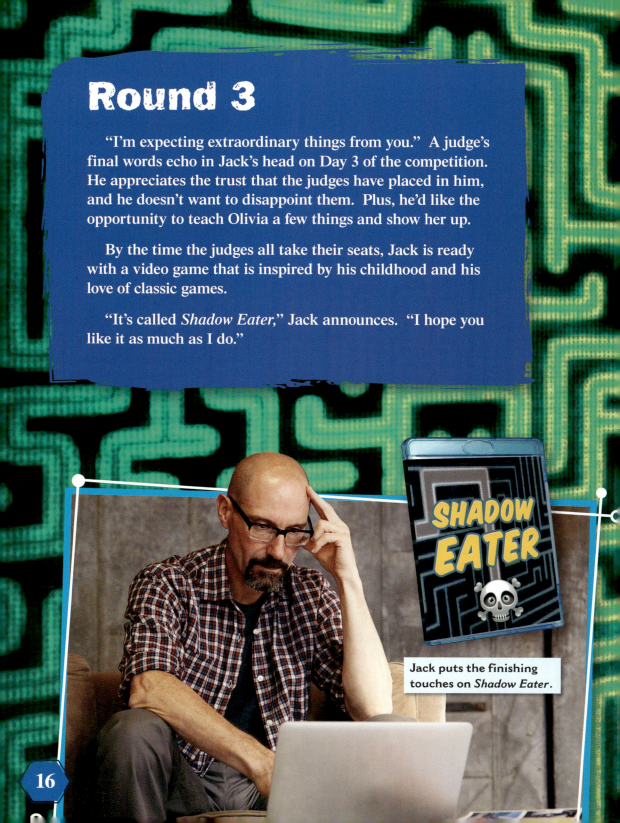

SHADOW EATER

Jack puts the finishing touches on *Shadow Eater.*

The crowd watches as the judges take control of a simple black skull that swallows darkness wherever it goes, leaving behind a trail of light. The screen becomes brighter and brighter as the judges navigate a series of mazes. There are squares inside of squares, twists, turns, and dead ends. Wrong turns prompt game controllers to vibrate a warning, and smart moves send the camera ahead to give players a sneak peek at upcoming parts of the maze.

"You've created a really uplifting experience, Jack," the panel concludes.

"It's not too old-school for you?" Olivia asks.

"Well, let's see what you have for us before we say any more," one judge responds.

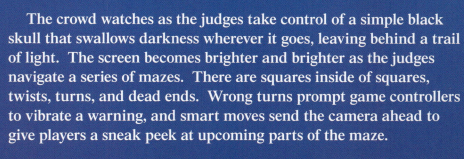

LET'S EXPLORE MATH

Shadow Eater has players navigate mazes made of squares. Are the following statements about squares always true, sometimes true, or never true? Justify your answers using words or pictures.

1. Squares have 4 right angles.
2. Quadrilaterals with 4 right angles are squares.
3. Squares are rectangles.
4. Quadrilaterals with 4 equal sides are squares.
5. Squares are parallelograms.
6. Squares are not polygons.

Olivia passes a headset to the judge and says, "Don't get your hopes up because this game is exceedingly simple."

As the judges settle into virtual reality, a stack of rectangular bricks appears on the screen. The audience immediately lets out a low groan. The setting has few colors. There is no music, no characters—but there also aren't any rules.

Olivia pushes on. "Welcome to *Terrestrial*."

"What is this place?" one judge asks.

"What you create is up to you," she replies as he picks up a brick. Then, he stomps on it and breaks it into four more bricks. He assembles the smaller rectangles on top of a larger pile of bricks. The audience claps politely while he keeps playing, but it's clear that they're bored.

But, the judge's reaction is more encouraging to Olivia. "I feel like I'm six years old again," he whispers.

He is mesmerized as he builds skyscrapers, amphitheaters, and monuments with the help of technology. Finally, he takes off the headset and says, "Congratulations" with a grin to Olivia.

Olivia had won the round, but the audience had no idea why.

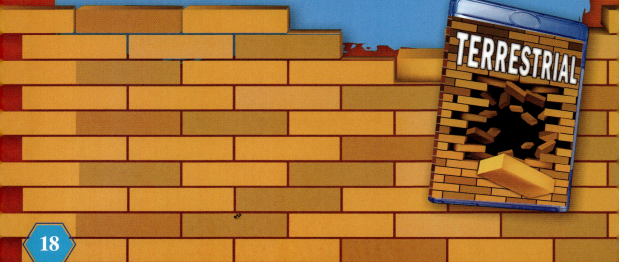

That night, the designers trade notes before leaving the convention.

"You're making this old man look bad," Jack jokes.

"Thanks, but I really like *Shadow Eater.* It feels like players can do something **virtuous**, rather than just rack up points."

"It doesn't take a genius to design a maze. *Terrestrial* wasn't just a game—it's a whole universe!"

"I had fun designing it, but I wish I knew why people like it so much. It's insanely simple—too simple. The judges shouldn't be this impressed."

"Simple, yes, but I'm going to let you in on a little old-school secret," replies Jack.

Olivia cringes, as she replies, "Yeah, sorry about that. You're definitely not old-school, but you're experienced, like a sushi master, or a professor, or um…."

Olivia and Jack plan for the next day.

Jack chuckles as he says, "People love creating worlds, and with *Terrestrial*, you turn players into designers who have total creative control."

"Maybe too much control. Didn't you see that he gave up?"

"He gave up when his vision was too creative for the tech. He couldn't figure out how to make his vision a reality."

"I will definitely make the next game easier to use," states Olivia.

"Elegant, creative, and easy to play? You're going to make *Terrestrial* look old-school!"

Olivia grins as she waves goodbye.

21

Round 4

"I was dreaming about *Terrestrial* last night," the judge confesses the next day.

Olivia laughs. "I can't seem to get it out of my head, either."

"Thank you for all you have brought to this competition," the judge says as he turns to the crowd. "And thank you to all who have advised me and the panel this past week. As you remember, Jack won the first round, but Olivia came back strong to win the **subsequent** rounds. So, she will present her final design first."

Olivia passes headsets to the judges, and soon, the screen is ablaze with strange shapes and colors.

"This is *Polygon Palace*." She raises her voice as the audience begins to chitchat. "Imagine a futuristic zoo filled with exotic animals made from polygons. There's a kinet that eats vibrations, a horax with an **ultrasonic** neigh, and a nibbler that builds a nest out of confetti."

The creatures gracefully bow their heads, inviting the judges to pet them. They are amazed. "I've never been anyplace so beautiful," one judge says.

"There isn't enough money in the world to create the places Olivia can imagine," Jack says.

She gives him a wink. "I can't wait to see what you've imagined."

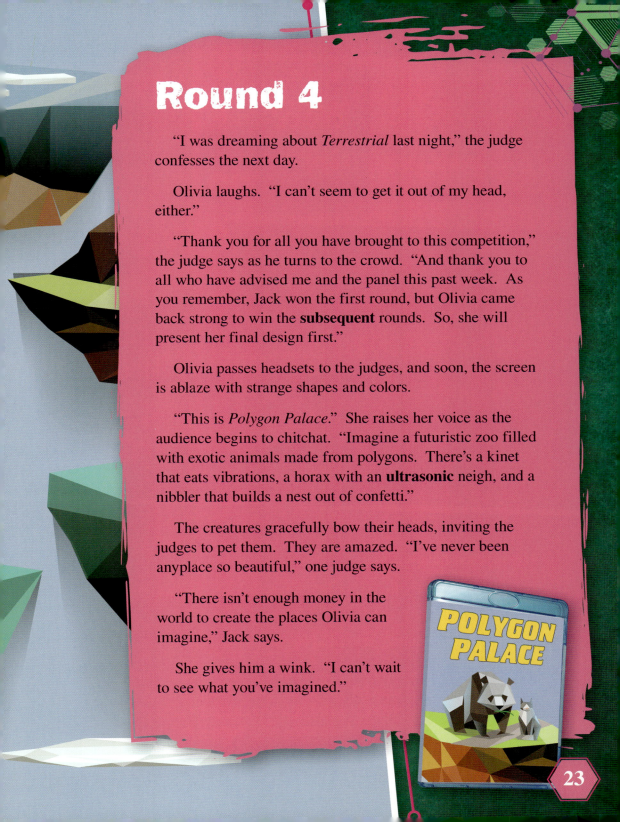

POLYGON PALACE

The audience is stunned to the point of silence. Judges reluctantly remove their headsets and switch to Jack's controllers.

Then, Jack starts his game, and a happy song chirps to the audience: *Meep, moop, meebo…Mishmashterpiece*!

A judge immediately grins and says, "This looks like fun."

She quickly scrolls through the panels on the screen, which are filled with polygons of every shape and color. Soon, she is mixing and matching shapes to create a series of loopy characters. She builds robots with rainbow feet and monsters with eight-sided heads.

In *MishMashTerpiece*, players use polygons to design characters. Design two robot characters: one using only parallelograms and the other using only quadrilaterals that are not parallelograms. Choose one quadrilateral from each character and explain why it is or is not a parallelogram.

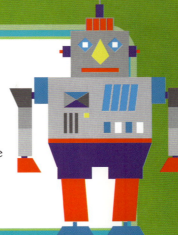

"All the better to balance on," she says. There is even an alien that resembles a **dodecagon**.

Olivia elbows Jack gently. "Hey! You stole my move."

"What do you mean?" questions Jack.

"You made a video game that lets players control their world."

The judge agrees, "That he did, and I can create a digital version of everyone I know—and everyone I wish I knew!"

"What can I say? People like people more than flying, mastering a maze, or exploring underwater worlds. They really just want to create characters that can be their friends, so they can compete together," Jack replies.

And the Winner Is...

"Jack, it's clear you are a master designer," a judge says. "You have used your vast experience with 2-D games and what you've learned from Olivia to create games that people will want to play."

Jack takes a quick bow, and then the judge continues. "Olivia, thank you for not holding back. You brought all your creativity to this challenge, and it showed. You have both created more than simple challenges for players. You've mastered the **elusive** art of creating feeling and designing worlds that don't need points, music, or levels to engage players. The characters, setting, movements, and other details you've developed make your games feel alive—"

Olivia interjects, "So...who is the winner?"

"This competition has proven that virtual reality has amazing potential. But, it is clear that the best 3-D designs rely on the same principles that make 2-D games successful. There will always be a place for these video games. This panel has decided that we would be honored to have both of you represent the organization as this year's winners."

"This is a win-win for both of us!" Jack exclaims.

"There's no other designer I would want to share this with," Olivia agrees.

LET'S EXPLORE MATH

The competition grouped games into two categories: 2-D and 3-D. Sort the polygons below into two categories of your choice. Explain how you sorted the polygons.

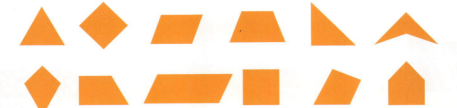

⚙ Problem Solving

Design a 2-D video game that uses polygons and the same principles Jack and Olivia rely on to make games fun. Sketch a storyboard of your game. Polygons can be used as icons, parts of the setting, characters, or other design elements. Write a short summary about how the game is played. Be sure your game includes at least two different examples of each of the following polygons:

- triangles
- quadrilaterals
- pentagons
- hexagons

Jack and Olivia's Tips and Tricks

- People play longer when they feel like they are making progress.

- Players enjoy games that feel as exciting as a roller coaster.

- Sound effects, lights, and motion engage players.

- Games should be easy to navigate.

- Controls should be simple to master.

- Levels should teach players new skills, test those skills, and then expand those skills.

- Games can be simple and open-ended if they offer players the chance to be in control.

Glossary

2-D—short for two-dimensional; having only two dimensions; flat figure

3-D—short for three-dimensional; having or seeming to have length, width, and depth

amphitheater—a round building with a large, open space in the middle used for games and performances

ascend—to climb or move upward

crystalline—clear and bright

designer—a person who creates a new product, including the way it looks and operates

dodecagon—a polygon with 12 sides

elusive—hard to understand

emcee—host of a show or ceremony

emits—to send out light from a specific source

interstellar—located or traveling among the stars

logo—a symbol a company or group uses to identify itself

mesmerizing—spellbinding or fascinating

portfolio—the collection of someone's work

principle—a general or basic truth on which other theories can be based

subsequent—happening after

ultrasonic—sounds that are too high-pitched for humans to hear

virtuous—having or showing moral goodness

Index

adjacent, 15

avatar, 10

camera, 17

circle, 15

controllers, 9, 14, 17, 24

designer, 4, 10

gamers, 7

headset, 10–12, 18, 24

hexagon, 28

maze, 17, 20, 25

moon, 10

parallelogram, 15, 17, 25

polygon, 17, 25

portfolio, 10

progress principle, 9

quadrilateral, 9, 15, 17, 25, 28

rectangle, 15, 17–18

screen, 10, 17–18, 23–24

speed games, 9

square, 17

triangle, 28

virtual reality, 7, 18, 26

Answer Key

Let's Explore Math

page 7:

square, rectangle, triangle, trapezoid

page 9:

B, E, F

page 15:

Examples of parallelograms: parallelogram, square, rectangle; Non-examples of parallelograms: kite, trapezoid

page 17:

1. Always true; all squares must have 4 right angles.

2. Sometimes true; rectangles also have 4 right angles.

3. Always true; all squares have 4 right angles and 2 pairs of opposite, equal, parallel sides like rectangles.

4. Sometimes true; rhombuses also have 4 equal sides.

5. Always true; all squares have 2 pairs of opposite, equal, parallel sides like parallelograms.

6. Never true; squares are quadrilaterals with 4 angles and 4 closed, straight sides, making them polygons.

page 25:

Characters will vary but should include one example using only parallelograms and the other using quadrilaterals that are not parallelograms. Explanations will vary but should include descriptions of parallelograms as quadrilaterals with 2 pairs of opposite, equal, parallel sides and how the quadrilaterals that are not parallelograms do not have all of these attributes.

page 27:

Sorts will vary. Examples may include polygons with right angles and polygons with no right angles, or quadrilaterals and polygons that are not quadrilaterals.

Problem Solving

Game summaries will vary but should include a description of how the game is played. Storyboards will vary but should include at least two different examples of each polygon (triangles, quadrilaterals, pentagons, and hexagons).